A SOLDIER'S PRAYER POEMS

Maximiano M. Reade

DEDICATED TO:

EUGENE BAESA READE

AND

LORETTA PONCE READE

MY PARENTS

WHO BOTH LIVED,

AND

LOVED BY EXAMPLE

ACKNOWLEDGEMENTS

IN SPITE OF WHAT
SOME PEOPLE MAY SAY,
IT IS NEVER TOO LATE
TO PUT PEN TO PAPER!
THIS BOOK OF POETRY
IS ALL ABOUT YOU!
IT IS ALSO ABOUT ME.
AFTER ALL, WITHOUT YOU,
THERE IS NO ME!
WITH THIS THOUGHT IN
MIND, I WANT TO THANK ALL
OF THOSE PEOPLE, POETS ALIVE
AND DEAD,
WHO HAVE SOLDIERED ON
IN MY JOURNEY.

Contents

Contents

NO MATTER

OUR WORLD IS FULL OF
WONDERFUL MYSTERIES,
PERHAPS THE GREATEST OF
THEM ALL IS MAN'S MIND.
WITHOUT MAN'S MIND,
THERE IS NO MATTER.
KNOW YOUR MIND.
LIKE YOURSELF.
YOU WILL BE AT PEACE WITH
YOURSELF AND WITH THE
MYSTERIES OF THE UNIVERSE.

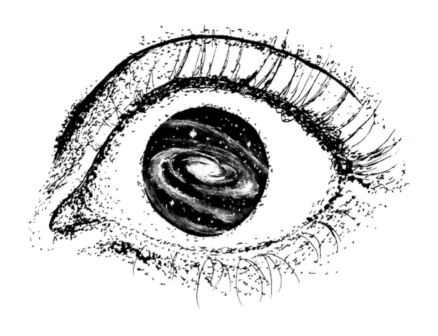

DANCING WATER

DANCING WATER,
NATURE'S FOUNTAIN,
WINTER'S FROST,
EMBRACING MOUNTAIN.
WATERFALLS CALM
SOOTHSAYER'S THRASHINGS,
A YOUNG FAWN'S GRACE,
A LION'S LASHINGS.
THE NORTHWIND SOARING
GENTLY IN THE SKY,
SUDDENLY FURY BASHING,
ONLY GOD KNOWS
WHY!

A CHILD'S LOVE

EXCUSE ME, EXCUSE ME PLEASE,
BE AT EASE. THE OCEAN SWAYING,
THE WIND IN THE TREES.
GOOD MORNING, SIR, I SO DECREE.
OUR WORLD SHOULD LIVE IN HARMONY.
DISSUADE THE PRESENT, AND BURY
THE PAST,
MOTHER TOLD ME OUR WORLD
WOULD LAST.
GROWN-UPS DUE, GROWN-UPS DIE.
CHILDREN, THE APPLE OF MY EYE,
A MAN, MY FRIEND, IS NONEXISTENT.
A CHILD'S LOVE SO, SO INSISTENT.

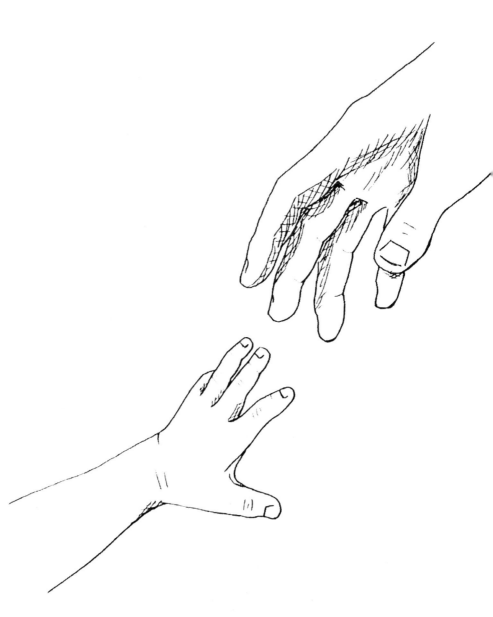

KENNEDY'S DEATH

LINCOLN'S ADDRESS
BROUGHT TOGETHER
NORTH AND SOUTH
TO HONOR HIM
AT REST
NO MATTER WHAT
RACE, COLOR, OR CREED.
THE NATION OF AMERICA
NOW STANDS AT HIS FEET.
BE PROUD AMERICA.
A GREAT MAN INDEED.
HE FOUGHT FOR HIS COUNTRY.
HE DIED FOR ITS CREED!
AS HE LIVES IN MEMORY,
MAY HE REST IN PEACE.

THE FOLLOWING TWO POEMS

WRITTEN IN SPANISH

ARE DEDICATED

TO THOSE WHO HAVE

SERVED AND LOST THEIR

LIVES IN SERVICE TO

OUR GREAT COUNTRY

REGALO

ES MI PAÍS
ES MI RAZÓN
ES MI AHIJADO
MI CORAZÓN.
TU REGALO
SOMBRERO DE ORO
BOTAS Y AMOR.

ALOHA AMOR

ALOHA AMOR,
CABALLERO DE BASTÓN
MOVIMIENTO CON RAZÓN.
CON TUS CUADRILLES Y TUS OJOS
ME ROBASTE EL CARAZÓN.
LINDA NIÑA, CERCA A DIÓS,
ENTRE LOS DOS ME HICIERON PEÓN.
VIRGEN LUPE, VIDA Y VOZ,
NUNCA TE DIRÉ ADIÓS.
ALOHA AMOR.

FEAR, SHOCK, JOY

FEAR, SHOCK, JOY,
ARE BUT STIMULANTS TO THE ACTION.
FEAR
MAY DRIVE YOU TO TEARS,
BUT
MAY ALSO DRIVE YOU TO COURAGE!
SHOCK
MAY DRIVE YOU TO INSANITY,
BUT
MAY ALSO DRIVE YOU TO REALITY!
JOY
JOY IS OUR INHERITANCE,
THE ACTION AND BARE EVIDENCE,
OF A MOMENT WE MAY YET RELIVE.
THANKS
TO OUR AMERICAN HERITAGE!

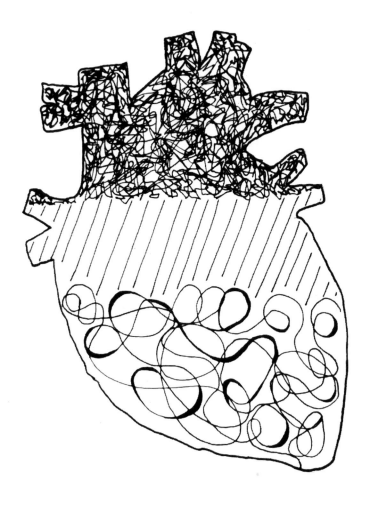

WHO ARE YOU?

YOU ARE EVERYTHING
THAT IS ANYTHING TO ME.
YOU ARE THE MOON,
YOU ARE THE SUN,
YOU ARE THE BEAUTY OF THE SEA.
YOU ARE SO, SO DEAR TO ME!

BLUE

BATTLE WEARY, MONSOON DREARY.

BUD DIED HARD, NOT ENOUGH TO BURY.

MYCA VILLAGE ACROSS THE WAY,

WHAT'S SAY WE REST AT CAM RANH BAY?

FINALLY, REST!

AND AS I LAY AND THINK,

OF HOME I PRAY

MY SON WON'T

BE ALONE THIS WAY.

IN SLUMBER

I FIND YESTERDAY'S BATTLES

FOUGHT IN MIND AS IF I HEAR

OLD SARGE SAY,

"BLOW, BLOW THE SCUM AWAY."

PEACE, AN ETERNITY AWAY,

PEACE AND ETERNITY SOMEDAY.

RED DRAGON SLAYER

ON A WING, A HORIZON.

IN MY HEART, A PRAYER.

MY LAST NAME'S MEDINA,

I AM A RED DRAGON SLAYER!

I AM CATHOLIC BY BIRTH,

CHRISTIAN BY NAME.

I CONFESS, NO WINGS,

BUT I AM NOT TO BLAME!

MY LAI, A NIGHTMARE,

MY WIFE CAN'T SLEEP.

THE ANSWER LIES DORMANT,

AND GOD, SO DEEP!

I PRAY

THE MONSOON CLEANSES

MY BECKONING CALL.

LET US PRAY,

GOD'S MERCY ENGULFS US ALL!

WHY TOM?

JOE: "THE VIET CONG HAD MY TWENTY,
WHY DID I ESCAPE THE MANY?"
MAX: "A RECURRING DREAM, THE THEME
THAT LED TO MY FRIENDSHIP
WITH OLD JIM BEAM!"
MAX ANSWERS JOE'S QUESTION WITH
A QUESTION
MAX: "THE VIET CONG HAD MY TWENTY,
HOW DID I ESCAPE THE MANY?"
JOE: "EACH NIGHT I RUN THROUGH
THAT JUNGLE...STEW!"
TOM: "IT'S ABOUT BOTH ME AND YOU."
YOU SEE, STEW WAS AMONG THE MANY,
THE VIET CONG HAD HIS TWENTY TOO!

24

TRACERS

TRACERS FLY LIKE DAGGERS IN THE NIGHT,

LIQUOR FLOWING, WINTER'S BITE.

MONSOONS FURY, PURE DELIGHT,

SUICIDES LINGER IN THE NIGHT.

AND

IN SPITE OF OUR NATION'S BLIGHT,

IT WAS NEVER OUR NATION'S FIGHT.

ASK THE KOCH BROTHERS, THEY'RE
ALWAYS RIGHT.

BUT

DEAD YOU MIGHT BE IN A FIREFIGHT.

"KEEP THE COKE IN THE BOTTLE"

SNIPER

EXCUSE ME,
EXCUSE ME, PLEASE!
SNIPERS IN THE TREES!
AT EASE,
P.T.S.D.
A DISEASE.
HOW LONG WILL THE RICH
KEEP US ON OUR KNEES?
FRIENDLY FIRE A REPRIEVE,
HE TRIED TO HELP
ON THE FIRING LINE
PLEASE,
READY ON THE RIGHT,
READY ON THE LEFT,
READY ON THE FIRING LINE!
SNIPER OR PIED PIPER?
EXCUSE ME, PLEASE!

27

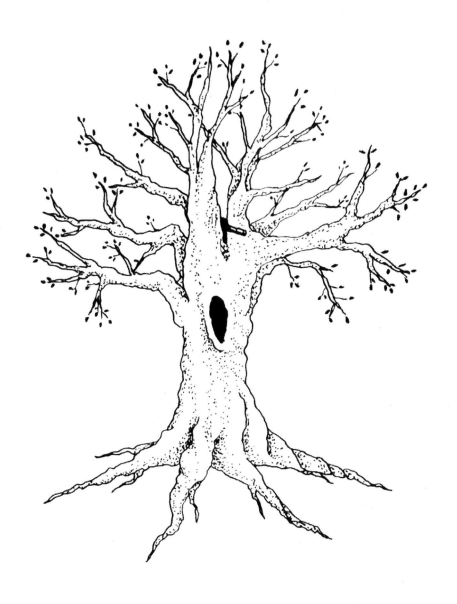

BITTERSWEET

AGAIN, LIFE MOURNS ANOTHER
BEAUTIFUL DAY,
BIRDS OF A FEATHER
STATUES OF CLAY.
DARKNESS DILUTED BY LIGHT AS IT MAY,
WHISPERING WILLOWS,
MARSHES THAT SWAY.
AGAIN, LIFE MOURNS ANOTHER
BEAUTIFUL DAY.

SILENT SOLDIER

JUST ANOTHER SILENT SOLDIER,

CAME BACK WOUNDED,

SO MUCH OLDER.

JUST TWO STRIPES UPON HIS SHOULDER.

SHE IS MY SISTER,

HE IS MY BROTHER,

THEY ARE MY HEROES,

SILENT SOLDIERS!

FALSE PRIDE AND SUICIDE

FALSE PRIDE BE DAMNED, MY FRIEND,

P.T.S.D. JUST AROUND THE BEND.

THE PAST IS IN THE PAST,

WHAT WE HAVE,

OUR THOUGHTS AND FALSE PRAYERS

WILL LAST.

DAMN FALSE PRIDE AND SUICIDE,

EMOTIONS TRIED AND TRUE ABIDE,

DAMN, DAMN, SUICIDE!

FALSE PRIDE BE DAMNED, MY FRIEND,

P.T.S.D. JUST AROUND THE NEXT BEND.

EMOTIONS TRIED AND TRUE ABIDE,

FORGIVE ME, MY SUICIDE!

LAUGHTER

PLEASE ABIDE,

AS TO WHO WE ARE,

LAUGHTER,

TEARS OF JOY!

LAUGHTER,

FROM BOTH NEAR AND FAR,

LAUGHTER,

A PRECIOUS COMMODITY!

BOTH NEAR AND FAR,

LETS US KNOW JUST WHO WE ARE!

NEW-FOUND SLAVE

FROM CRADLE TO GRAVE,
THERE'S A NEW-FOUND SLAVE.
A SLAVE TO THE MARKETS,
A BRICK AND MORTAR SLAVE.
FROM DAWN TO DUSK,
AND DUSK TO DAY,
THERE'S A NEW-FOUND SLAVE!
FIFTEEN DOLLARS AN HOUR,
NOT A LIVING WAGE.

TRIBES

PLEASE UNDERSTAND
WE ARE ALL THE SAME, FOLKS
PLEASE UNDERSTAND
WE'RE ALL GOING INSANE, FOLKS
WE'RE ALL THE SAME, FOLKS
WE'RE ALL INSANE, FOLKS
PLEASE UNDERSTAND
WE'RE ALL THE SAME, FOLKS
WE'RE JUST DIFFERENT BLOKES!

ANTI-MATTER

I DON'T KNOW,
AND IT DOESN'T MATTER.
WHEN I FALL,
I WILL ONLY SPLATTER.
SHOULD HAVE USED A LONGER LADDER
AND
A DIPPER FOR MY BLADDER.
SHOULD'A, WOULD'A, COULD'A
HAD HER
NOW IT REALLY DOESN'T MATTER.

SPIRIT LODGE

WHO KNEW HOW TO ENJOY
THE MOUNTAIN AND THE DEW,
ENDURE THE FRACTURED WINTER BLUE?
WHO, WHAT, WHEN, WHERE?
THE BLOKE WAS NEITHER HERE, NOR THERE.
PINK ELEPHANTS FLYING EVERYWHERE.
WHO KNEW HOW TO ENJOY
THE SPIRITS AND THE FAIR,
BREATHE IN THE HUSKY MOUNTAIN AIR?
RESPECT THE SPIRITS AND BEWARE.
WHO, WHAT, WHEN, WHERE?
SHOUT OUT ALOUD! THE SPIRITS SPARE
THOSE WHO KNOW HOW TO WINTER THERE!

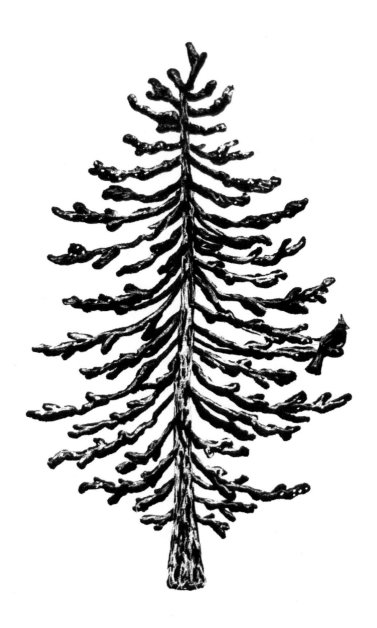

THE END OF MY JOURNEY

THE END OF MY JOURNEY
WILL BE THROUGH THE FRONT DOOR.
THE BACK DOOR TO MY JOURNEY
HAS SHUT, TIGHT.
I CAN NO LONGER WITHDRAW FROM
MY FEARS OR MY DELIGHTS.
MY JOURNEY IS NOW
TOWARD THE LIGHT.
ALL I CAN SAY IS
HANG ON TIGHT!

WAIT FOR THE OPEN GATE

LIFE IS LOSS

LIFE IS CHANGE

LIFE IS LOVE

LIFE IS BLAME

LIFE IS HATE

AND AS WE WAIT

LIFE SHOULD BE

AN OPEN GATE!

DNA

MY DNA

A FRAGILE BLOWN

GLASS

A RARE AVOCADO

MASS

WRAPPED UP

IN A YELLOW RIBBON

THAT WILL

PASS

FROM THE FUTURE

INTO THE PAST!

JUST LIKE THE

ART THAT'S IN THE

LASS

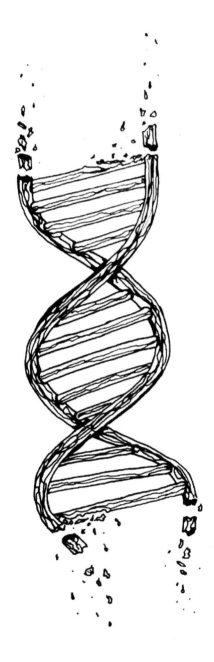

INDEED

EXCEPTIONAL MY FRIEND,
INDEED.
EXCEPTIONAL MY FRIEND,
NO NEED.
MEDIOCRE, QUITE A JOKER,
MAKES A LIVING PLAYING POKER.
AN ACE IN HAND,
A DARING STEED,
MY FRIEND,
THE RUMMY'S NAME
IS READE.
A STRUTTING HEART
IN WORD AND DEED,
INDEED!

IN MY DREAMS

IN MY DREAMS,

IN THE THRONE OF MY DREAMS,

YOU ARE THE BEAUTIFUL QUEEN OF
MY DREAMS.

I'VE BEEN TOLD OF ANGELS AND SPIRITS
THAT SPEAK,

OF MANSIONS OF GOLD ABOVE THE
BRIGHT SKIES.

BUT THE ANGEL I LOVE, AND SPIRIT I SEEK,

IS THE ANGEL OF LOVE IN YOUR
BEAUTIFUL EYES.

THE SPIRIT I SEEK IS THE CHEER OF
YOUR FACE,

WITH ITS BEAUTY AND LIGHT AND
MAGNIFICENT GRACE.

WHILE THE MANSION OF GOLD IS AN
EXCITING TREASURE

I VALUE YOUR FRIENDSHIP ABOVE
DEAREST PLEASURE.

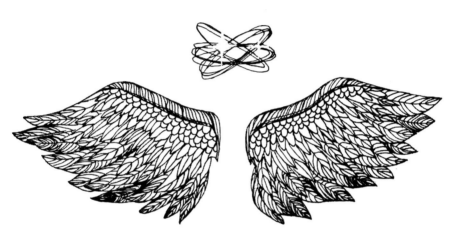

IN MY DREAMS WAS PENNED BY
MILTON DANIEL READE THE II.
IT WAS FOUND
IN A PUBLICATION OF HIS WORK IN 1921.

THE ILLUSTRATOR

Grace Otto is a 17 year-old high school senior who lives in Utica, New York. Grace began her interest in art at the age of 11. She enjoys using different mediums to include charcoal, oil, watercolor and graphite. Born into a military family, Grace has lived in Texas, Washington, Kansas, Maryland, Colorado and eight years in Germany. Being a part of this book has been a great honor, especially because of her appreciation for those who have served and currently serve in the military. Her goal is to attend the Pratt Art Institute in Utica and eventually own her own art gallery. Artwork inquiries and commission requests can be made at icantbeadisgrace@gmail.com.

GRACE OTTO

THE AUTHOR

This book of poetry is the work of a lifetime, Max's lifetime. Now 74 years old, Max started writing poetry when he was ten years old. His only goals in writing poetry were to explore his emotions and "have fun." These two goals are his hope for you, the reader, to get in touch with your thoughts and feelings, and, also, to have fun.

Born in Deming, New Mexico, in 1946, Max and his family moved to El Paso, Texas, when he was four. His father found work on Ft. Bliss as a plumber. Max grew up with his older sister, Mary Jean and his younger brother, Guadalupe, or "Lupe." He attended a Catholic elementary school where reading did not come easily to him. He discovered later that he was dyslexic.

His father died when he was nine years old; initially, his poetry was dark. He was fascinated with Edgar Allen Poe, not the subject so much, but how it flowed. As he grew older, he studied the naturalist Henry David Thoreau.

Max graduated from Burgess High School in May 1966. He joined the U.S. Air Force from 1966 to 1970, and earned the rank of Sergeant. After having served in Vietnam, he returned to the states and graduated from the University of Texas at El Paso with a Bachelor of Science degree in Criminal Justice. While employed in a number of jobs, because of his PTSD, he continued to work on his poetry. Max currently lives in El Paso, Texas. (email: makiereade4@gmail.com)

Max feels poetry lives closely to music, song writing, theater, and literature. He was very fortunate to have been introduced to Grace Otto, an emerging new artist, literally on the scene. The book cover and pages of his poetry are illustrated by Grace Otto with her visual impressions of his writing. Both the poetry and the art are fun to see, read, reflect on and enjoy.

MAXIMIANO M. READE